A CHEYENNE SKETCHBOOK:
Selected Poems 1970–1991

*For
in poetry
in peace*

NYC
09

A CHEYENNE SKETCHBOOK:
Selected Poems 1970–1991

by Lance Henson

The Greenfield Review Press
Greenfield Center, NY

ISBN 0-912678-62-3

Revised 2nd Printing 1992

Library of Congress Number 85-70355
Greenfield Review Chapbook #62

Printed in the U.S.A.

Cover Art by Robbie McMurtry

The Greenfield Review Press
Greenfield Center, NY 12833

Acknowledgments

Poems in this collection are selections from five books published between 1970 and 1984. The books are out of print. Each poem has been published at least once in a small press magazine or anthology. The books listed respectively are:

Keeper of Arrows, Renaissance Press, Chickasha, Oklahoma
Naming the Dark, Point Riders Press, Norman, Oklahoma
Mistah, Strawberry Press, New York
Buffalo Marrow on Black, Full Count Press, Edmond, Oklahoma
A Circling Remembrance, Blue Cloud Quarterly, Marvin,
        South Dakota

Small press magazines in which these poems have appeared include:

Nimrod, Shaman, Coyote's Journal, Dacotah Territory, Prairie Schooner, Scarab, The Greenfield Review, Blue Beech, Whisperings of the Wind, Harvard Magazine, Tulsa University Magazine, Contact II and *Territory of Oklahoma*.

Anthologies include:

Carriers of the Dream Wheel, Harper and Row
Voices of the Rainbow, Viking Press
The Remembered Earth, University of New Mexico
Songs From This Earth On Turtle's Back, Greenfield Review Press
The Written, Spoken and Unspoken Word, University of Oklahoma
        Press
American Indian Literature, University of Oklahoma
        Press
Voices in the Blood, New American Library
The Grat Plains Poetry Anthology, Point Riders Press, Norman,
        Oklahoma
The Clouds Threw This Light, Institute of American Indian Arts
        Press

for the cheyenne

Contents

winter day near calumet

frost has thickened
over the screen
grey clouds pass through
the field into the
january sky

bits of brown fur
are caught on the
wood near the shed

old ones have
passed here

winter back

the old rest among forest grey

somewhere
grandmother you whisper
a name that was never born

circles of mist gather a
moment against this breath
on the window

then disappear

bay poem

where from the watch towers
the rust of
shipwrecks
shine

bar
where the sailor
remembered
peace and
laughed

epitaph soaked
sponges
across bars

endless
       damp
streets

lovely moonshine
at
       2
       am
on the edge
of
rain

impressions of the peyote ritual

oh heavenly father
bless us your children
as we sit around the
red earth moon

hear us now as we
turn to your face
look behind our words
as we pray

give us what is pure
bring us from the half sound

heal us from our wounds

father

i call you from within the gourd sound
i call you from my smoke
i call my whole self which lives in you

you answer from everywhere

holy spirit of no place
forever soul

pity me
give me
light

prairie wind
let your midnight
song find me among
blessed ones

bone flute
sound of humanity
show me how i may
better know my
mother earth

sound of my father
          i
              pray
bring peace to all
                  cheyenne

great spirit
now we are one
long have we suffered
without your wisdom

our water
corn
we share with you

rope of leather

river
                brother sun

dusted eagle wing
sweet prairie medicine
comfort me your lonely son

i listen to the river of
ghosts and weep for my
brothers who call through
the wind

maheo

it is good to see you
sitting among them

our smoke has gone four ways
it calls for us

my brothers smile with tears
we may never meet again

eagle of fire whose
wings are scented cedar

moon of forever who
guards the sacred seed

keep us strong
to meet the
coming days

celebration

a cold light
at the edge
of words

our hands
shivering
with sleep
reach toward
the moon

the chairs stand
alone near the
table

in a portrait
a woman is holding her
apron

catching the
snow

seeing

a dry limb
knocks all day
at the wind

and i have been
here before
though the roots of
things flow around
me without
touching

when i look i see
that even
now

i am crossing
the same
endless
bridge

wrapped in
a strange garment

looking for
myself

old country

we are forgotten in the year
resigned to pale rooms

like stale bread we sit in the damp
familiar to the rain on the roof

on the street in early morning
someone is singing

an old lady in a shawl
with a basket
is calling the name of
a lost cat
come home

come home

song of myself

1
i am without an echo

there is a small light
like a whisper on the
leaves

and my love is in this
place

the ashes drift

the rain runs through her
laughter

2
i follow the embering sun
far into the trees

the wind breathes damp as a
cellar

3
i come upon the gifts of the old
and the stars are weeping

there is a portrait dying in
my eyes

4
i am alone near the lake on a december
night without
a coat
sipping
coors
and
crow

anniversary poem for the cheyennes
who died at sand creek

when we have come this long way
past cold grey fields
past the stone markers etched with the
names they left us

we will speak for the first time to the season
to the ponds

touching the dead grass

our voices the colour of watching

portrait in february

near chanute kansas
snow with rain splashes the windshield

a barn through evening haze stands alone
in a frozen field

it is the last snow before spring
a redbird huddles on the barnsill

farther on
near an ice edged pond an owl
sits watching
as we pass

on our way home

sitting alone in tulsa
three a m

round dance of day has gone

a sirens scream splashes the blinds like ice
a fly sits frozen on a yellow plastic cup
the end tables huddle in pairs

sale at renbergs on ladies shoes
          felt squares and soft knits at the mill outlet

whatever i have done today has gone without me

the edges of the city and the pale moon reflect
in the same river

how easily we forget

warrior nation trilogy

1
from the mountains we come
lifting our voices for the beautiful
road you have given

we are the buffalo people
we dwell in the light of our father sun
in the shadow of our mother earth

we are the beautiful people
we roam the great plains without fear
in our days the land has taught us oneness
we alone breathe with the rivers
we alone hear the song of the stones

2
oh ghost that follows me
find in me strength to know the wisdom
of this life

take me to the mountain of my grandfather
i have heard him all night
singing among the summer leaves

3
great spirit (maheo)

make me whole
i have come this day with my spirit
i am not afraid
for i have seen in vision
the white buffalo
grazing the frozen field
which grows near the full circle
of this
world

commanche ghost dance

we will return to life
we will stay in the sun long before the shadows
    are borne

there will be no distance between our words and
    the banished moon

in all that grows while the winter reaps
we will live again

poem for carroll
descendant of chiefs

again the call of the winter birds

among the domino men
        in a must filled room
                there is talk of thieves

in a broken house the risingbears
        watch the old man roll a cigarette

shadows of his smoke curl yellow against
        the ragged paper curtain

while the bone moon
        watches from a windless sky

we are a people

days pass easy over these ancient hills

i wander near a moccasin path overgrown with
rusted cans and weeds
i stand in the forest at sunset waiting for
a song from the rising wind

it is this way forever in this place
there is no distance between the name
of my race
and the owl calling
nor the badgers gentle plodding

we are a people born under symbols
that rise from the dust to touch us
that pass through the cedars where
our old ones sleep

to tell us of their dreams

morning star*

in the wallow that morning with only scattered
rounds
not a word passed

yet
near the end the old women stopped chanting
lifting their broken hands they stood

listening it is said to the laughter of children
in the cold
howling
wind

---

*cheyenne chief dull knife's sioux name
 a remnant of cheyennes died escaping after being held
 captive at fort robinson nebraska 1878

mistah

you come upon an incurable distance

a crow flies into the
day lit moon

the journey that was your calling
escapes

in the field
i am calling toward a house
in which
no one lives

at chadwicks bar and grill
oklahoma city

a sky the color of a wrens breath
hangs over red clouds
hint of rain
and home is dirt underfoot
tu fu and li po have
forgiven nothing
not waking drunk under any moon
or the incessant calling
of a loon
so waiting is the roses own
signature
the spider catches the fly
at morning
whether i am there
or not

poem in july

water falls from the cup of a hand
late the moons silhouette behind clouds

wind in this hour
is the sound of a young girls dress

mist on the hair of her arms
her face a sudden petal
in matchlight

trees cross the fields alone
windrows of new mown hay

a bird flies into her sleep
scent of rain

the wind pauses
knowing she is sky

two calendar days from winter

in a lampless room
steam rises from a clay cup
and disappears

at the door
the wind is saying goodbye
as it nestles in the curled hand
of a child asleep

silence like a gray tear
falls from my grandfathers house
this snowless day

north

north of my grandfathers house
shadows of first winter storm walk
the fields toward the north canadian

without a word
the prengant dog i have tried
to be rid of for weeks
has gone

in the house my daughter
has disappeared into
dream

her small trembling hands
flower into a cold wind that smells
of the moon

marys poem

day grows dark
violet as the veil of a childs dream
threads of years woven in clouds of rain

a patchwork quilt on the bed in late afternoon
from the ceiling a mobile of ornate bells
circles slowly

looking back across fields of fog
you remember a wintry afternoon
where you stood long hours in front of the mirror

quiet sister
one bell shivers into sound

buffalo marrow on black

wind of sage in which the world dreams
       strike the earth where i have walked
              let my relatives hear this

scent of cedar pass tonight over the faces of the
sleeping
       world and the paths of the sick and troubled
       and weak

brother sun
       help me to be remembered among all
           growing things

sister water
       grandfather fire

                        muts i mi u na
                        wo is ta
                        henah haneh
                        henah haneh

buffalo calf road woman
       buffalo woman
           this is all
              this is all

song for warriors

for bill dunnam

just west of watonga
after hours of beers at fats place

my friend stops the car
i walk to the carcass of badger
and cut one claw
from a front foot

lost in a blur of road and coors
i feel a deeper loss
in the scent
in the the blessing on my hands

near the wichita mountains

caught between two dreams
the moons thin presence looms in reddening dusk

an eagle talon tied with sinew hangs from the
mirror of the jeep
under a star quilt of sky
this somnolent gaze of winter flows through
us like a slow country song

cold pieces of light tap the windshield
as we move west
over frozen ground

autumn birds

pigeon in a stained glass window
sky the color of a splash of quail
in the house
in the middle of evening
a girl sits at a table on whose cloth
seagulls turn in october

a crescent moon over darkened fields
damplight falls on stacked tipi poles
wind of night
the flight of autumn birds

evening song

outside a whisper moves wind like
through the trees
sunlight drifts over the yard

a slow circumference
        where the world is green

a white bird flies through the light of someone
missing

i have watched a long time
        from the window of this old house

all that i have lost is here
        the world fills with its presence

dusk this evening
prairie light through a red shawl

rain in april 81
lake murray state park

for pat

it rains
the landscape of my heart searches for you
a gray rain falls into my shadow

how long these leaves stuck to my window
how long before the click in my head
leads me from the black butterfly
to light

day is a ribbon faded
                          shape of a flying bird
            dawn mist

from a journal entry
riding near calumet

nightwind warm for early january
a slow ride misted windows
the farms in oklahoma are old men
most with vacant eyes
waiting for messages

we hear the ticks of rain on the window
the clock flips to eleven thirty eight
the car heaves sliding from sleep

the room

for my son

a child wakes up thirsty
pulls back the curtain where the blue light stays
the fields white and alone
ache with the song his eyes know

in this deepest of evenings
under his window
tracks of starlight

snow makes a fable of the wasted garden
in the breadth and resin
of a cold time

for gene leroy hart

the wind has thrown wide the door
to sam pidgeons shack

he sits in morning light remembering
that a man without a spirit runs the loneliest road

owl calls over the din of footsteps
                              the laughter in bars

a brown wind pauses among spider webs

five poems for coyote
from cheyenne country

1
he is rust
            in moonlight

2
when the roadman paused
                        we heard our brothers voice

3
in snow
        one track

4
eight without ears
hang upside down from fence posts
near hammon oklahoma

5
the moonlight splashes
in their
eyes

untitled

ohkom nivas hatamah
crazy horse and snake on bear butte
make the wind whirl around the prayer ribbons

in the canadian river valley
near calumet oklahoma
i heard the high moan the singular voice
of coyote

so alone
my shepherd would not rise to answer

ohkom maheo shiva domni
warrior heart
moon in the still lake of dream

this night i hold my hands out to you

song in autumn

washed aside by solemn days
shadows of things reach toward us
spoon and cradle
prism and flower
hand that reaches through another hand
the darkened grasp

small solitudes resound in our words
and we realize
the shadows they leave behind

memory is the shadow that stays

vision song

the scent of sage and sweetgrass
braids
a man saying goodbye
to himself

for my grandfather

the wind brushes the window
looking for the world

i am looking for you

the afternoon falters

a mourner gathers her scarves and lamp
the streets empty

toward the narrow landscape
i taste in my glass

a cemetery of stars

haiku at rock creek

tishomingo oklahoma

a ritual of crows
            just after dawn

      mosquitos
            peyote moon

at the ramada inn

an aquarium of popcorn
bursts from visions of miss emilys
picture
just inside lawton at one fifteen
in the morning
it bourbon and seven
the tables are a shiny tin
whisper
the juke box occasionally skips
four miles distant
on a windy cemetery hill
a stone eagle that marks geronimos
grave
rises into the night
if i had to name this hour
i would hold it up to the light
and ask to be
something more

near midway truck stop

along the turner turnpike at a rest stop
between oklahoma city and tulsa
i feel the morning sun inch over the leaves of
    a small elm
rising to the scent of sage and wildflowers i lean
    on one
elbow

beyond the field the sound of cars and a lone
    water tower
mark a small town
i remove the knife from under the sleeping bag
and place it in the sheath on my hip

ho hatama hestoz na no me*
it is july
i imagine coffee in a pale cup on a wooden table
far from here
and look west toward home

---

*there is a powerful trembling around me

impressions of the cheyenne way

1

it is dawn
pity the names we have spoken
touch these feathers that have flown
your road

grandfather cedar
i am picking up your ways

2

maheo walks among us
in a wind of sage the world
is dreaming

scent of water
the smoke has circled

i am looking for your face

3

our father
maheo

i send my song
the darkest sinew of my life

pity me
this night opens on my small spirit

i am alone

dusk in august

everywhere while the sun sets
you burst into bloom

three white mushrooms in the last glint of sun
the rattle of night beginning in the stone

there are letters written so deeply
so delicately upon the burnt face of evening

and i found them
while everything changed

while the path where i stood grew from the ground
and followed the birds west in crimson light

12/28/87

above the glittering cold of lund sweden
a sky
clear and vast
as a line from transtromer*

late winter

the earth frozen and still
dreams of sunlit
wheat

---

*tomas transtromer, the renowned swedish poet

wo he iv* 11/29/90

the rain lays down
beside
a fallen leaf

a crow
flies overhead carrying
a bright piece of string

for the first time this day
i will speak your name

waiting the night through

for the morning
star

---

*morning star, michael wayne henson's cheyenne name
 born on the day and exact time of the sand creek massacre 1864

this afternoon looking for my grandmothers words
i remember a half eaten pear browning
on her window sill

and her telling me about the stones i had brought
her from europe singing inside her dreams

i see her folding the brightest days
of her life
into a small buckskin square

her sorrow colored days
have become this gray michigan sky

her quiet strength
the smallest white flower
in a field

from the edge   4/21/91

a leaf falls through its shadow
the ashes of afternoon
flow past

the hour is a shadowgame only the desperate
can feel
columbus' people angry and alone in their
    sickened dreams
america
it is a lie

my child sleeps
breathing in the wounded air

Lance Henson is a member of the Cheyenne Nation and an accomplished poet. He was born and raised among his tribe in Western Oklahoma. He holds a master's degree in Creative Writing from the University of Tulsa which he attended as a Ford Foundation scholar. He is an ex-marine, a member of the Cheyenne Dog Soldier Society, the Black Belt Karate Association, and the Native American Church.

Mr. Henson has published 14 books of poetry, five of which were published by European presses. His work has been included in most major anthologies of Native American literature including *Songs From This Earth On Turtle's Back* and *Harper and Row's Twentieth Century Anthology of Native American Poets*.

Lance Henson has worked as a poet-in-residence in more than 800 schools in the United States and Europe. He has read and lectured to university, gallery and community audiences and on reservations. In August of 1988 he addressed the United Nations Conference on Indigenous People in Geneva, Switzerland. His work has been translated into more than 15 languages including Russian, French, and Italian. Mr. Henson recently collaborated on an album of rock music and spoken poetry recorded in Pisa, Italy. He recently collaborated with a playwright/composer on a musical theatre piece based on the Sand Creek Massacre. It was produced off-Broadway in February of 1991.

Mr. Henson is currently working in the Albany, NY area public schools for the Alternative Literature Programs in the Schools (ALPS) as a writer-in-residence.